All rights reserved. No part of this book may be reproduced, stored in a retrieval system or transmitted, in any form or by any means, mechanical, photocopying, recording or otherwise, without any prior written permission of the publisher.

© B. Jain Publishers (P) Ltd.

Published by Kuldeep Jain for
Pegasus
An imprint of
B. JAIN PUBLISHERS (P) LTD.
An ISO 9001 : 2000 Certified Company
1921/10, Chuna Mandi, Paharganj, New Delhi 110 055 (INDIA)
Tel.: +91-11-4567 1000   Fax: +91-11-4567 1010
Email: info@bjain.com   Website: **www.bjain.com**

Printed in India by
J.J. Offset Printers

PEGASUS ENCYCLOPEDIA LIBRARY

Sports
TENNIS

Edited by: Pallabi B. Tomar, Hitesh Iplani
Managing editor: Tapasi De
Designed by: Vijesh Chahal, Anil kumar
Illustrated by: Suman S. Roy, Tanoy Choudhury
Colouring done by: Vinay Kumar, Kiran Kumari & Pradeep Kumar

CONTENTS

What is tennis? 3

Tennis equipments 6

Tennis court 7

The game 10

Scoring 12

Umpires 15

Shots 16

Governing body 17

Major events 18

Other forms of tennis 20

Tennis legends 21

Test Your Memory 31

Index 32

What is tennis?

Tennis is a racquet and ball sport that can be played both outdoors and indoors. The rectangular space it is played on is known as a tennis court. A tennis court is divided into two equal halves by a low net.

The aim of the game is to score points by hitting the ball over the net into the opponent's side of the court in such a way that the opponent is unable to reach it and hit it back. It is played between two players or two teams of two players each.

Tennis is a very popular game played at all levels of society and by people of varied age groups. Anyone who can hold a racquet can play tennis.

Astonishing fact

People in wheelchairs can also play tennis and special tournaments are held for them.

TENNIS

The beginning

The origin of tennis, like any other sport, is disputed. However, it is popularly believed by experts that the game originated in French monasteries in the 11th century. French monks played a game similar to handball against the walls or over a rope tied across a courtyard.

Astonishing fact

The name tennis comes from the French word 'tenez' (from tenir) which means 'take this'. The monks used to yell 'tenez' at their opponents as they hit the ball with their hands.

The modern version of tennis was invented in December 1873 by Major Walter Clopton Wingfield in Wales. On the basis of the older sport of indoor tennis, Major Walter devised a game for the entertainment of his guests in his estate.

Indoor tennis, or real tennis, as it was called, is originally derived from the same game played by the French monks in 11th century.

What is tennis?

Singles match

A singles match takes place between two players competing against each other. The two players can be either two men or two women or even one man against one woman.

Doubles match

In a doubles match there are two teams of two players each. Teams are of single gender that is all-male or all-female.

Mixed doubles

Mixed doubles is played between two teams consisting of one male player and one female player each.

Astonishing fact

Canadian doubles match is played with 3 people - one person against a doubles team!!

Tennis equipments

Racquets

A tennis racquet consists of a handle and a neck joining an oval shaped head that has a network of tightly pulled strings. Initially, racquets were made of wood and their strings of animal gut. Now, racquets are made from materials like graphite, titanium, carbon fibre etc., to give them strength and lightness.

Modern tennis racquets vary in length, weight and head size. An average racket is about 28 inches long and weighs about 284-397 gm.

Tennis ball

Tennis balls are hollow rubber balls with a fuzzy, felt coating. According to the International Tennis Federation (ITF), the diameter of tennis ball should be 2.5-2.7 inches and must weigh between 56 to 59 grams. The United States Tennis Association (USTA) and ITF allow only yellow and white colours. However, most balls produced are fluorescent yellow in colour. This colour, also called optic yellow, was first introduced in 1972.

Astonishing fact

The best quality racquets are sold without strings, as experienced players prefer to decide what strings should be used with the racquet and with how much tightness they should be strung!!

Tennis court

Tennis court is a rectangular, flat surface, usually covered with grass or clay. However, concrete and carpet surfaces are used as well. It is 23.77 m long, and 8.23 m wide for singles matches and 10.97 m wide for doubles matches. Carpet surface is used for indoor matches.

A net is stretched in the middle of the court, dividing it into two equal halves. It is 1.07m high at both ends, and 0.914m high in the centre.

Astonishing fact

Major Wingfield's original court had the shape of an hourglass!! It was narrowest at the centre.

The design of the modern tennis court is based on the tennis court designed by Major Walter C. Wingfield in 1873. Since then, tennis court has undergone many changes and assumed its present format.

TENNIS

Lines

The lines at the farthest ends of the court are known as the baselines. They define the width of the court. The short mark in the centre of each baseline is referred to as either the hash mark or the centre mark.

The outermost lines to the left and the right of the players that make up the length of the court are called the doubles sidelines. These lines are used as margins when doubles matches are played.

The lines to the inside of the doubles sidelines are used as boundaries for singles matches and are known as singles sidelines.

> **Astonishing fact**
> The Falkland Palace Royal Tennis Club is the oldest tennis court in use today.

The area between these two lines (doubles and singles sidelines) is available for play only during doubles matches and is called the doubles alley. In other words, when doubles matches are played, the doubles sideline are taken to be the boundaries of the court.

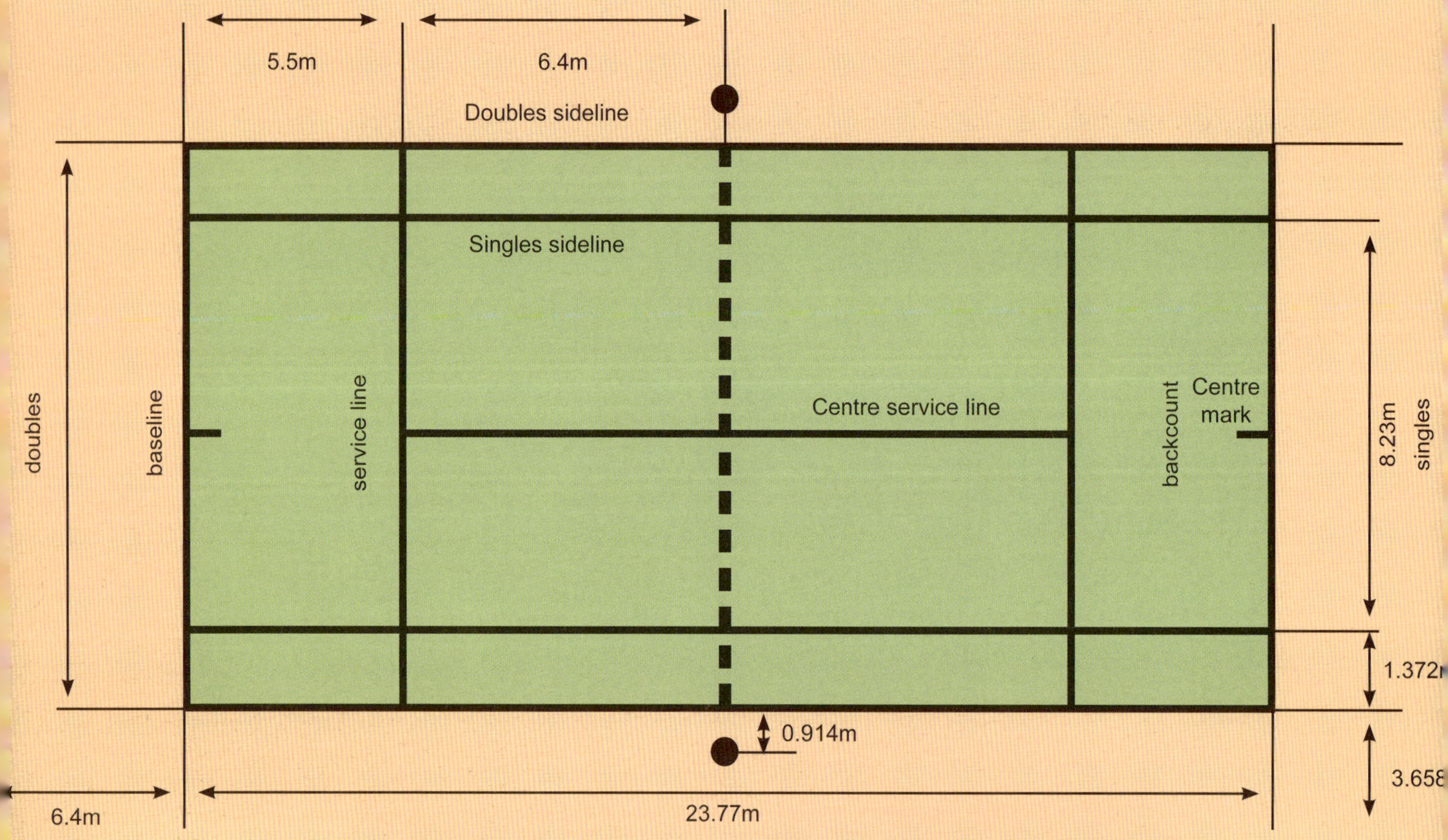

Tennis court

The line that runs between the net and the baseline is called the service line. It is called so because the server must be able to hit the ball in such a manner that the ball lands into the area between the service line and the net on the receiving side. The area between the baseline and the service line is known as back court.

The centre line runs parallel to the sidelines and divides the service line in two equal parts. As a result of which, two rectangular boxes of equal size are formed; these are called service boxes. While making a serve a server has to make sure that the ball lands into the diagonally opposite box of the receiver.

A ball is considered 'out of play' only if it goes outside the court without coming in contact with the boundary lines or the area inside the lines upon its first bounce.

Astonishing fact

Steffi Graf defeated Natasha Zvereva in only 32 minutes in the shortest ever French Open match in 1988.

The game

To play, players position themselves on the opposite sides of the net. One of the players is made the server, and the opposing player, the receiver.

The server makes the shot from behind his baseline, standing somewhere between the centre mark and the sideline. The receiver is allowed to stand anywhere on his side of the net. The server hits the shot whenever the receiver is ready.

The ball must reach the opponents' diagonally opposite service box across the court in such a way that it does not touch the net. However, it is essential that the ball travels above the net during all shots.

Net (or let) service

If, on its way to the opponents' side, the ball touches the net and then lands in the service box, then this is considered a void serve and the server must make the serve again. Such a serve is known as let or net service. Let service is not considered as a fault and the player can serve any number of void services in a point.

Faults

If a hit falls out of the valid service box (diagonally opposite), or if it fails to clear the net then it is considered as a fault. A foot fault occurs when a player's foot comes in contact with the baseline or with the centre mark before the ball is hit. If the second serve also incurs a fault then it is considered a double fault, and the opponent wins the point.

If a proper service is made, then the players hit the ball continuously across the net. This is called a rally. After the ball falls on their side of the court the players must hit the ball before it has bounced more than once. The player or team will lose a point if they fail to hit the ball back into the opponents' court.

At the end of the first and every odd-numbered game, the players switch ends of the court, and the player who served the previous game now receives serve.

Scoring

Scoring in tennis is very different from the rest of the games. A tennis match is composed of points, games and sets. First of all, one must score four points to win a game. Then, after winning six games one wins a set. However, the winner must win at least two more games than his opponent. And finally, one must win two, or sometimes three, sets to win the match.

Love, fifteen, thirty and forty

In tennis, the four points are called by different names. The score of zero is called love. The first game point is called fifteen. The second game point is called thirty, and the next or third game point made is called forty. After forty, one more point is required to win the game. As the player wins the fourth point, it is called game.

Therefore, if the score is 'fifteen-love', it means that the server has scored one point in the game while his or her opponent has not scored any point yet and therefore has a score of zero. The score is written as '15-love'.

Astonishing fact

Love comes from the French word 'l'ouef' which means egg!!

Scoring

When both the players reach an equal score during a game, then the score is: '(score of the server)-all'. For e.g. '15-all'

When both players have won three points in a game the score is described as deuce. To win in such a condition, one of the players must win two points more to win the game.

The player who wins the next point after deuce is said to have the advantage. If the advantage player loses the next point, the score becomes deuce again. On the other hand, if the player with the advantage wins the next point, than he wins the game, since the player is now ahead by two points.

Astonishing fact

The first round match between the Nicolas Mahut and John Isner at the 2010 Wimbledon is the longest tennis match ever played. It lasted 183 games and took 11 hours and 5 minutes to finish!!

TENNIS

Score calls

Normally, the scores in a tennis match are announced by the umpire. However, if there is no umpire, then the server has to announce the game score before he serves. A server is supposed to announce his score first. For example, if the server loses the first three points of his service game, he would say, 'Love, 40.'

Before serving for the first game of the next set the server announces the set scores so far completed in the match. If he has won two sets and is beginning the third, he would say, 'two love, new set.' If he had lost the first two sets, he would say, 'Love, two, new set.' At the end of the match, when either of the players is asked the score, the player announcing the score announces his scores first. For example, if a player declares that the score of his match was 6–4, 2–6, 3–6, it means that he won the first set but lost the next two sets. This will mean that the he has lost the match too.

Astonishing fact

The scoring system in a tennis game (15-30-40) is said to have derived from the four quarters of a clock with one quarter representing 15 minutes and the next 30, and so on!!

Given below is a table showing the point scores and the corresponding calls that a server or the umpire would make before playing a shot in a formal match.

Point score	Calls
3 – 4	advantage out
4 – 3	advantage in
4 – 4	deuce
4 – 6	game
5 – 3	game

In case of a tie at the score of 6–6, another game is played called a 'seven point tiebreak.' The set is won by the player who not only wins at least seven points in the tiebreak but also scores two points more than his opponent. For example, if the score is 6 points to 5 points and the player with 6 points wins the next point, he wins the tiebreak game and the set. However, if the player with 5 points wins the game, the tiebreak will continue till the time one player is two points ahead of the another player.

Astonishing fact

At the age of 16 in 1997, Martina Hingis became the youngest women's tennis player to be ranked number 1 in the world since the rankings began in 1975.

Umpires

A tennis match is presided over by an umpire who sits in a raised chair on one side of the court. The umpire has absolute authority to make factual judgements regarding the game.

The umpire is also assisted by line judges who decide whether the ball has landed within the boundaries or outside it and whether the player has committed a foot fault or not. There also maybe a net judge who determines whether the ball has touched the net during service.

The umpire is also assisted by line judges who decide whether the ball has landed within the boundaries or outside it and whether the player has committed a foot fault or not. There also maybe a net judge who determines whether the ball has touched the net during service.

The referee is the ultimate authority on tennis rules. The referee may overrule the umpire's decision when called to the court by the players. However, he cannot change the umpire's decision regarding a fact. But when the referee is present on the court during the play, then he can completely overrule the umpire's decision if he sees a violation or misjudgement in his decision.

Astonishing fact

John McEnroe once yelled at an umpire, 'You cannot be serious!'

Shots

Professional tennis players generally employ a large number and variety of shots in their game. Below are described some of the most popular shots. The shots have been described for the right handed players.

> ### Astonishing fact
> The fastest serve ever recorded was made by Andy Roddick in the 2004 Davis cup. It was measured at 155 miles per hour!

Types of shots

The **serve** is made for the first point of the game. In a serve the player first tosses the ball in air and then hits it at its maximum height. A few advanced players usually try to hit a winning shot with their serve. Forehand stroke begins at the right side of the body and moves across the body towards the left side.

A **backhand** stroke begins on the left side of the player's body and moves across it ending on its right side. It can be executed with either one hand or with both. A **volley** is made in the air before the ball makes its bounce near the net. A **half volley** is made by hitting the ball immediately after it has bounced. This shot too is made near the net. The **lob** is used by a player when he finds himself in a poor defensive position on the baseline. The ball is hit high and deep into the opponent's court to either to provide the lobber (the player who plays the lob shot) the time to get into a better defensive position or to win the point by hitting it over the opponent's head.

The **drop shot** is employed if the player finds his opponent standing far behind in his court. The ball is tapped softly just over the net so that the opponent is taken by surprise and is unable to run in fast enough to return it back. An **ace** is a serve which is hit with such a great force that the opponent is unable to return it thereby losing the point.

Governing body

> **Astonishing fact**
>
> Believe it or not, in the first Wimbledon tournament the tickets were sold for one shilling each in the final match!

The International Tennis Federation (ITF) is the governing body of international tennis. It has 205 national tennis associations.

The ITF was originally established as International Lawn Tennis Federation (ILTF) by 12 national associations at a conference in Paris, France on 1st March 1913. Later on in 1924, the ITLF became the recognised official authority to control lawn tennis throughout the world and for the first time official rules of tennis were formulated. In 1977 the ILTF removed the word 'Lawn' from its title.

The ITF moved its offices to London during Second World War.

TENNIS

Major events

Grand Slam Tournaments

The Australian Open, the French Open, Wimbledon, and the US Open together form the Grand Slam tournaments. They are also known as the Majors. These tournaments happen every year and are the most important events in tennis.

If a player or a team wins all the four tournaments in the same year, that team or player is considered to have won the Grand Slam. If they manage to win the four tournaments one after the other but not in the same year, then it is known as a Non-Calendar Year Grand Slam. A Career Grand Slam means that a player has won all the four tournaments in different years in his entire career.

The most prestigious accomplishment for a tennis player is the Golden Slam which involves winning all the four grand slam tournaments and the gold medal at the Summer Olympics in the same year. The only player to achieve the Golden Slam till now is Steffi Graf. She won it in 1988.

Astonishing fact

The French Open is also known as the Roland-Garros, named so after Roland Garros, a world-famous aviator and World War I flying ace.

Australian open

French open

Wimbledon

US open

Major events

Davis cup

The Davis cup is an international team event in men's tennis held annually. Players representing their respective countries compete against each other. It is organised and managed by the International Tennis Federation (ITF).

Fed cup, earlier known as the Federation cup, is the women's counterpart of the Davis cup.

The Fed cup was known as the Federation cup till 1995. The cup was launched to mark the 50th anniversary of the International Tennis Federation. in 1963.

Davis cup

Hopman cup

The Hopman cup is another important international team event held annually in Perth, Western Australia in early January or sometimes in late December. Mixed teamsthat is teams composed of both male and female players, from various countries compete with each other. It is also known as the ITF Mixed Teams Championship.

Hopman cup

Masters 1000

The ATP World Tour Masters 1000 is a series of nine tournaments each of which is held annually. They are the second most important event in men's tennis. A win at one of these events grants a huge leap in rankings to the player. The series was formerly known as 'Super Nine'. Later on, they came to be known as the Tennis Masters Series. The finals of this series are held in November at the end of the tennis year, called the ATP World Tour Finals.

Other forms of tennis

Paddle tennis: In paddle tennis, the court used is smaller than the regular tennis court and has no doubles lanes. The net is lower than that of standard tennis game. It is played with a solid paddle instead of a strung racquet and a depressurized tennis ball. The same court is used for both singles and doubles.

Real tennis: Real tennis is the original indoor racquet sport from which the modern game of lawn tennis originated. It is also known as court tennis in the United States royal tennis in Australia and courte-paume in France.

Canadian doubles: Three players play in a Canadian doubles with a single player on one side and two players on the other. The single player hits into a doubles court while the side with two players hits into a singles court.

Australian doubles: This is an informal type of tennis match which has yet to be accepted by the authorities. It is played with rules similar to Canadian doubles with the exception that players rotate court position after each game. As a result each player gets the chance to play both singles and doubles. The singles player always serves in an Australian doubles.

Jordache tennis: Jordache tennis is played between three players. First two players play a match. Players are awarded 5 points for a game win and the loser is awarded points based on the score achieved: 3 for deuce, 2 for 30 and 1 for 15. The winner remains on the court. The loser leaves the court and is replaced by the third player. The first player to score 50 points wins.

Wheelchair tennis: Wheelchair tennis is played in both singles and doubles by people in wheelchairs. The ball is allowed to bounce twice before it is hit. The second bounce can even be outside the court. All the four Grand Slam tournaments include wheelchair tennis.

Tennis legends

ROD LAVER

Country:	Australia
Career titles:	76
Tennis hall of fame:	1981
Status:	Retired

ACHIEVEMENTS:

Grand Slam title wins:

Australian Open:	in 1960, 1962, 1969
French Open:	in 1962, 1969
Wimbledon:	in 1961, 1962, 1968, 1969
US Open:	in 1962, 1969
Grand Slams:	1962, 1969

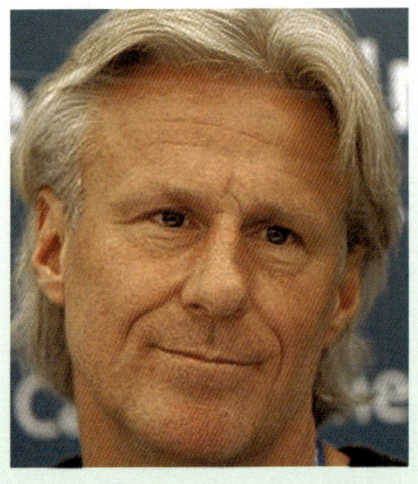

BJORN BORG

Country:	Sweden
Career titles:	100
Tennis Hall of Fame:	2003
Status:	Retired

ACHIEVEMENTS:

Grand Slam title wins:

French Open:	in 1974, 1975 1978, 1979, 1980, 1981
Wimbledon:	in 1976, 1977, 1978, 1979, 1980
ATP World Tour finals:	In 1979, 1980

TENNIS

PETE SAMPRAS

Country:	United States
Career titles:	64
Tennis Hall of Fame:	in 2007
Status:	Retired

ACHIEVEMENTS:

Grand Slam title wins:

Australian Open:	in 1994, 1997
Wimbledon:	in 1993, 1994,1995,1997,1998, 1999, 2000
US Open:	in 1990, 1993, 1995, 1996, 2002
ATP World Tour finals:	In 1991, 1994, 1996, 1997, 1999

ROGER FEDERER

Country:	Switzerland
Career titles:	63
Tennis Hall of Fame:	---
Status:	Active

ACHIEVEMENTS:

Grand Slam titles:

Australian Open:	in 2004, 2006, 2007, 2010
French Open:	in 2009
Wimbledon:	in 2003, 2004, 2005, 2006, 2007, 2009
US Open:	in 2004, 2005, 2006, 2007, 2008
ATP World Tour finals:	In 2003, 2004, 2006, 2007
Olympics:	Gold medal, in 2008 (doubles)

Tennis legends

JOHN McENROE

Country:	United States
Career titles:	99
Tennis Hall of Fame:	1999
Status:	Retired

ACHIEVEMENTS:

Grand Slam titles:

Wimbledon:	in 1981, 1983, 1984
US Open:	in 1979, 1980, 1981, 1984
ATP World Tour finals:	In 1978, 1983, 1984

IVAN LENDL

Country:	Czechoslovakia (1978–1992), United States (1992-)
Career titles:	144
Tennis Hall of Fame:	2001
Status:	Retired

ACHIEVEMENTS

Grand Slam titles

Australian Open:	in 1989, 1990
French Open:	in 1984, 1986, 1987
US Open:	in 1985, 1986, 1987
ATP World Tour finals	In 1981, 1982, 1985, 1986, 1987

John McEnroe was named 'Father of the Year' in the year 1996 alongside people like Robert F. Kennedy, Jr., Brian Williams etc.

TENNIS

JIMMY CONNORS

Country:	United States
Career titles:	148
Tennis Hall of Fame:	1998
Status:	Retired

ACHIEVEMENTS:

Grand Slam titles:

Australian Open:	in 1974
Wimbledon:	in 1974, 1982
US Open:	in 1974, 1976, 1978, 1982, 1983
ATP World Tour finals:	In 1977

ANDRE AGASSI

Country:	United States
Career titles:	68
Tennis hall of fame:	---
Status:	Retired

ACHIEVEMENTS:

Grand Slam titles (Career Grand Slam):

Australian Open:	in 1995, 2000, 2001, 2003
French Open:	in 1999
Wimbledon:	in 1992
US Open:	in 1994, 1996
ATP World Tour finals:	In 1990
Olympics (Career Golden Slam):	Gold medal, 1996,

Tennis legends

BORIS BECKER

Country:	Germany
Career titles:	49
Tennis Hall of Fame:	in 2003
Status:	Retired

ACHIEVEMENTS:

Grand Slam titles (singles)

Australian Open:	in 1991, 1996
Wimbledon:	in 1985, 1986, 1989
US Open:	in 1989
ATP World Tour finals:	In 1988, 1992, 1995
Olympics	Gold medal, in 1992 (doubles)

Boris Becker is the youngest player to win men's championship at Wimbledon. He was merely 17 years old when he won it!!

MATS WILANDER

Country:	Sweden
Career titles:	33
Tennis Hall of Fame:	2002
Status:	Retired

ACHIEVEMENTS:

Grand Slam title wins

Australian Open:	in 1983, 1984, 1988
French Open:	in 1982, 1985, and 1988
U.S. Open:	in 1988

TENNIS

JUSTINE HENIN

Country:	Belgium
Career titles:	43
Tennis Hall of Fame:	---
Status:	Active

ACHIEVEMENTS:

Grand Sam titles:

Australian Open:	2004
French Open:	2003, 2005, 2006, 2007
US Open:	2003, 2007
WTA championships:	2006, 2007
Olympics	Gold medal, 2004 (singles)

BILLIE JEAN KING

Country:	United States
Career titles:	129
Tennis Hall of Fame:	1987
Status:	retired

ACHIEVEMENTS:

Grand Slam titles:

Australian Open:	1968
French Open:	1972
Wimbledon:	1966, 1967, 1968, 1972, 1973, 1975
US Open:	1967, 1971, 1972, 1974

> In 1973 Billie Jean King beat Bobby Riggs in three straight sets after he challenged her to a match where he boasted of the superior abilities of the male athletes over female athletes. The match was held at the Houston Astrodome on September 20, 1973 and came to be called 'the battle of the sexes'.

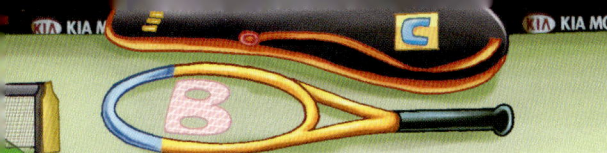

Tennis legends

MONICA SELES

Country:	United States
Career titles:	53
Tennis Hall of Fame:	2009
Status:	Retired

ACHIEVEMENTS:

Grand Slam titles

Australian Open:	1991, 1992, 1993, 1996
French Open:	1990, 1991, 1992
US Open:	1991, 1992
WTA championships:	1990, 1991, 1992
Olympics:	Bronze medal, 2000 (singles)

VENUS WILLIAMS

Country:	United States
Career titles:	43
Tennis Hall of Fame:	---
Status:	Active

ACHIEVEMENTS:

Grand Slam titles:

Wimbledon:	2000, 2001, 2005, 2007, 2008
US Open:	2001 2002
WTA championships:	2008
Olympics:	Gold medal, 2000 (singles), 2000, 2008 (doubles)

The fastest serve in women's tennis was recorded by Venus Williams in European Indoor Championships. The serve was done at a speed of 205 km/h!

TENNIS

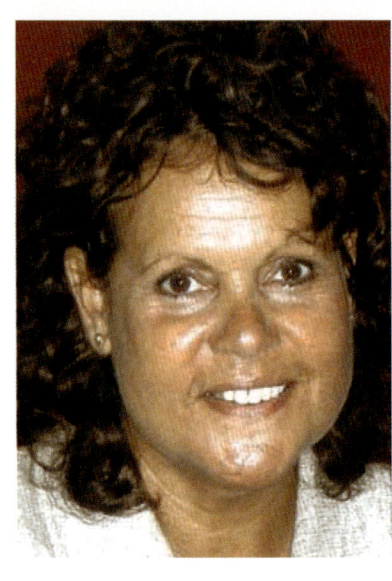

EVONNE GOOLAGONG CAWLEY

Country:	Australia
Career titles:	68
Tennis Hall of Fame:	1988
Status:	Retired

ACHIEVEMENTS:

Grand Slam titles

Australian Open:	1974, 1975, 1976, 1977
French Open:	1971
Wimbledon:	1971, 1980

STEFFI GRAF

Country:	Germany
Career titles:	107
Tennis Hall of Fame:	2004
Status:	Retired

ACHIEVEMENTS:

Grand Slam titles:

Australian Open:	1988, 1989, 1990, 1994
French Open:	1987, 1988, 1993 1995, 1996, 1999
Wimbledon:	1988, 1989, 1991, 1992, 1993, 1995, 1996
US Open:	1988, 1989, 1993, 1995, 1996
WTA championships	1987, 1989, 1993, 1995, 1996
Olympics	Gold medal, (singles), bronze medal (doubles) 1988, Silver, 1992 (singles)

Steffi Graf is the only tennis player to win the Golden Slam that is she won all the grand slam titles and the Olympic gold medal in a single year!!

Tennis legends

MARGARET COURT

Country:	Australia
Career titles:	192
Tennis Hall of Fame:	---
Status:	Retired

ACHIEVEMENTS:

Grand Slam titles:

Australian Open:	1960, 1961, 1962, 1963, 1964, 1965, 1966, 1969, 1970, 1971, 1973
French Open:	1962, 1964, 1969, 1970, 1973
Wimbledon:	1963, 1965, 1970
US Open:	1962, 1965, 1969, 1970, 1973

MARTINA NAVRATILOVA

Country:	Czechoslovakia, United States
Career titles:	167
Tennis Hall of Fame:	2000
Status:	Retired

ACHIEVEMENTS:

Grand Slam titles:

Australian Open:	1981, 1983, 1985
French Open:	1982, 1984
Wimbledon:	1978, 1979, 1982, 1983, 1984, 1985, 1986, 1987, 1990
US Open:	1983, 1984, 1986, 1987
WTA championships:	1978, 1979, 1981, 1983, 1984, 1985, 1986, 1986

The legendary Martina Navratilova has won the Wimbledon Women Singles 9 times which is the highest!

TENNIS

SERENA WILLIAMS

Country:	United States
Career titles:	37
Tennis Hall of Fame:	---
Status:	Active

ACHIEVEMENTS:

Grand Slam titles:

Australian Open:	2003, 2005, 2007, 2009, 2010
French Open:	2002
Wimbledon:	2002, 2003, 2009, 2010
US Open:	1999, 2002, 2008
WTA championships	2001, 2009
Olympics:	Gold medal, in 2000, 2008 (doubles)

CHRIS EVERT

Country:	United States
Career titles:	157
Tennis Hall of Fame:	1995
Status:	Retired

ACHIEVEMENTS:

Grand Slam titles:

Australian Open:	1982, 1984
French Open:	1974, 1975, 1979, 1980, 1983, 1985, 1986
Wimbledon:	1974, 1976, 1981
US Open:	1975, 1976, 1977, 1978, 1980, 1982
WTA championships:	1972, 1973, 1975, 1977

Test Your MEMORY

1. Who invented the modern version of tennis and when?
2. When was optic yellow, the standard colour for tennis ball first introduced?
3. What is the length of a professional tennis court?
4. How much score do you have if you score a 'love' in a tennis game?
5. How much score do you have if you score a 'thirty' in the game?
6. When was the ITF established?
7. What was the ITF originally called?
8. How many Grand Slam tournaments are there? Name them.
9. Who is the only player to win a Golden Slam?
10. In which event of tennis do mixed doubles team compete?
11. What is the other name for Grand Slam tournaments?
12. What is the other name for the Hopman cup?

Index

A

ace 16, 18

B

backhand 16
ball 3, 4, 6, 9, 10, 11, 15, 16, 20
baselines 8

C

centre line 9

D

deuce 13, 14, 20
doubles alley 8
doubles match 5
doubles sidelines 8
drop shot 16

F

fault 10, 11, 15
Forehand 16
forty 12

G

game 3, 4, 10, 11, 12, 13, 14, 15, 16, 20
Grand Slam 18, 20, 21, 22, 23, 24, 25, 26, 27, 28, 29, 30

H

half volley 16

L

lob 16
love 12, 14

M

Major Walter C. Wingfield 7
Mixed doubles 5

N

net 3, 7, 9, 10, 11, 15, 16, 20

P

points 3, 12, 13, 14, 20

R

racquet 3, 6, 20
rally 11
receiver 9, 10

S

Scoring 12, 14
serve 9, 10, 11, 16, 20, 27
server 9, 10, 12, 13, 14
service boxes 9

service line 8, 9
singles match 5
singles sidelines 8

T

Tennis 3, 4, 6, 7, 8, 9, 12, 13, 15, 16, 17, 19, 21, 22, 23, 24, 25, 26, 27, 28, 29, 30
tennis court 3, 7, 8
thirty 12

V

volley 16